Lady Balls Journal

THE OFFICIAL COMPANION
TO THE BEST SELLING BOOK

MINA IRFAN
THEUNIVERSEGURU LLC
HOUSTON, TEXAS

Lady Balls Journal\Mina Irfan - 1st ed.

ISBN: 979-8-9890423-1-9

To 7 generations back and 7 generations forward.
For Sheena and Alina.
For us.

TABLE OF CONTENTS

INTRODUCTION

Hello Beautiful!

You have picked up the official companion journal to my best-selling book, **Lady Balls: How to be Savagely Successful in a World Addicted to Suffering**.

In this Journal you will find quotes from the book, inner work journal prompts, affirmations, exercises and more. Journaling has been a huge part of my journey and I highly recommend it for both men and women. Putting pen to paper not only has energetic benefits in decluttering our thoughts and feelings, it can also help us channel messages from our subconscious and the divine quantum field. What's more, writing has been scientifically proven to aid in memory and the retention of important information.

It is highly recommended that you read the **Lady Balls: How to be Savagely Successful Book** alongside doing this journal.

Journaling

I journal every single day. Of course, some days I end up writing only a few sentences and other days I may fill up pages upon pages of things coming through me. I have never regretted journaling; however, it did take me a bit to get my groove with it.

There is no right or wrong way to journal. Just get started and you will discover what works for you over time. Use the journal prompts in this journal to get your juices flowing. I found it incredibly useful to use the same prompts over a period of days, weeks, and months to get deeper and deeper into my channeling. I do have my favorite prompts but I try to vary them a bit to get the most potent answers from within.

When journaling, try not to "think" as much as you feel or "flow." This can be tough in the beginning but I promise you will get the hang of it over time.

Affirmations

Affirmations are instructions to the subconscious. The key to reciting them is to say them with feeling. I usually use one or two a day and recite them throughout the day with as much feeling as I can muster in that moment. This immediately starts uplifting my moods. Saying them with high emotions is how we can reprogram our subconscious with these new beliefs.

Saying too many affirmations about various topics all in one day can actually take longer to program. Try and choose just one or two of your favorites and focus on them for at least a few days before trying a different one.

Invocations

Invocations are collaborative prayers with God. Instead of the usual begging type prayers most people do, invocations can form a relationship with the Divine while helping you reprogram with your subconscious mind at the same time! Talk about a win-win situation!

Invocations are most potent when recited around the same time every day for at least 21 days in a row. If you miss a day, it is best to start the 21-day count once again. I love to add an element of ritual to my morning invocations by lighting a candle and relaxing my body and mind into a semi meditative state. You can do this by focusing on your breath for a minute or two and then count out loud backwards from 10 to 1. Say the invocation with intention and feeling to get the best out of it. It is okay to go for longer than 21 days if you wish but try and do at least 21 days in a row daily within the same hour that you usually do them.

Lastly, I pray that these prompts, affirmations, and invocations transform your life like they have mine and the tens of thousands of my students before you.

Oceans of Love,
Mina Irfan

PART 1:

INTRODUCTION TO MINA IRFAN'S STAGES OF CONSCIOUSNESS

STAGES OF GODDESS EVOLUTION

As we have been learning in the Lady Balls Book, our DNA, womb wounds, and childhood conditioning all shape who we become. All this shapes our identity and how we show up in this world. I have developed a framework and tool to help myself and my students see where they are in their inner work journey and what next steps will help them most.

Basic Babe™
Self-Aware Barbie™
Million Dollar Babe™
High End Divinity™

These stages are meant to be used as a guide to help you select the best inner work tools and techniques for yourself. They are not meant to be weaponized against yourself or others. Please be kind and respectful of everyone's journey. Especially your own. I find most people to be a mixture of these 4 levels. It's best to think of these stages not as an on/off switch, but instead as a dimmer switch. A fluid continuum of stages and levels that we ebb and flow through.

Most people have one dominant stage where they spend the most time. Others have one stage and then fall into a lower stage when triggered. Which one is your dominant stage most of the time? And also, which stage is activated when you are triggered?

It may also be helpful to see each stage as split into three parts. With the third stage merging with the level above it. These stages can exist in percentages within the same person. For example, you could be 50% Basic Babe and 50% Self-Aware Barbie.

Basic Babe

A Basic Babe is in the wounded inner child stage. In this stage, one sees themselves as powerless and as victims to people, places, and circumstances. Entitlement can also be a huge issue in this stage. They can be very childish in their mental processing and reasoning especially when triggered.

People in this stage are dependent on others to get their basic physical and emotional needs met. From their point of view, someone else is held responsible for their survival and wellbeing. That someone could be parents, siblings, romantic partners, friends or the government.

The Basic Babe is the forever damsel in distress and massive victimhood. Everything is happening to the Basic Babe. She has no sense of responsibility and has given away her personal power to people, places, and circumstances. She is addicted to drama, complaining, and has low self-worth. She is often not receptive to love due to constricted heart center and low self-worth. Often addicted to drama, food, or gossip. Hoping to find a man to take care of her so she can go from mommy and daddy to someone else providing. A lot of her energy is used up in finding and keeping a man or drama with friends.

You are a Basic Babe, if you...

- Have trouble creating plans, structures, goals, and sticking to them.
- Have trouble making money and mostly rely on other people for manifesting things or money in your life.
- You are easily triggered and often lose control of your senses and emotions when in a triggered state.
- Feel like everyone is out to get you. It's always someone else's fault why you are not happy and successful in life.
- It always feels like you need someone else's permission before making even the simplest decisions in your life.

- Feel very dependent on others to get your basic emotional, physical, and financial needs met.
- Lack a sense of direction and purpose in your life.

If you relate to this, start your inner work immediately. I recommend finding a great therapist either in your area or online. You will need to do some inner child work and heal your mother and father wounds before advancing to the next stage. This will help activate your personal power and healthy masculine energy in your life. You can find additional resources in the resources section of this book.

Self-Aware Barbie

Self-Aware Barbie is the wounded masculine/feminine stage. This stage is activated when a woman's fight/flight response is turned on through life trauma or conditioning, putting the woman in her wounded masculine. This doesn't have to be something big like in my case. It could be as simple as growing up with a super masculine mother in a masculine society where achievements and structure are celebrated more than intuition and play. The Self-Aware Barbie takes personal responsibility for her triggers. In fact, she may overly blame herself even when it's not her fault! She catches her triggers and is actively working to rewire her neural pathways. She is taking back her personal power via hard work and determination. She is a go-getter, please-pleaser and over giver. Usually has an over-developed masculine side. Heart center is beginning to open as she becomes more receptive, especially in stage three. SABs are great at creating structures and disciplines for themselves and others.

An important thing to consider about SABs is that they activate the "predator" response in even generally good people. The truth is that most people are somewhere in the middle of the human vs divine spectrum. They are generally good but may choose to act questionably when the opportunity presents itself. Remember the saying, "Give them a finger and they will take a hand?" When the Self-Aware Barbie shows up knowing it all, doing it all, and giving it all, it awakens entitlement and even predatory behavior in others. I personally seem to have a PhD in awakening the "I am entitled to your time and energy" response from all kinds of people. I have seen countless fully grown, capable people act like they own me. This has been a continued journey of inner work on my part. If you deal with this, the tips in the following chapters will help you free yourself from this energy.

Self-Aware Barbie Phases

Phase one SAB is part Basic Babe and part SAB. She can get a job, make money, be resourceful, and independent when needed. However, she has a high addiction to drama and victimhood. She won't let any opportunity go for a good fight, argument, or text message battle. She sees herself being the victim even though the whole thing is often facilitated by her. She will often ask really disempowering and even childish questions. In this stage, our SAB has less structure and more chaos.

She is beginning to use her masculine energy to build something for herself. However, her feminine energy is still wounded and coming through in a disempowered, childish way. Going back to our fight or flight example, she is more fight than flight. Her drama extends from getting into comment wars on social media, group messaging battles with family and friends, and issues with co-workers and clients that limit her riches drastically!!

If there was a message I could give to the phase one SAB, it would be: Girl, stop it! You are stunting your growth and leaving money on the table. Use the techniques I shared in this book to give drama the boot once and for all! You are meant for riches and a divinely luxurious lifestyle. Drama has no room in your world, well, okay maybe in your bold outfit, but that's about it! It will always look like someone else is starting it since you have managed to collect drama addicted people around you. You will have to outgrew it fast and evolve out of it even if it means losing some friendships.

Phase two SAB is the information spitter. In this phase, the SAB is keeping herself busy and away from drama. She busies herself with her education and learning new things. Which is amazing and we are so proud of her! She gets obsessed with topics and literally gets a PHD in every topic she finds interesting. She is the queen at creating structures but not very good at getting into flow. The issue? She isn't embodying all of it yet but instead leaking energy by giving others unsolicited advice and coaching for free with her newfound information. Most of the people she preaches to, unfortunately, are not interested in learning something from a disembodied teacher. And because of this she often feels very unseen, unheard, and misunderstood.

In this stage, she is using mostly her masculine energy at the expense of her femininity. And for the record, this has nothing to do with how someone looks. You can be the most girly girl in your makeup and attire, and spend your entire day in your masculine energy.

Message for SAB phase two: God gave you this information for YOU. It's yours to keep, enjoy, and embody. This is not the time to share unless someone explicitly asks and better yet, exchanges money with you. Remember that complaining and venting are not invitations for advice. Most people don't actually want to change and will actually become resentful if you try to solve the problems they are addicted to. Use what you are learning for your own benefit. Once you fully embody it, the right people will be coming to you begging for your secrets.

This happened to me when I was diagnosed with rheumatoid arthritis in 2012. I refused medication and threw myself in 8 hours of daily study of nutrition and other lifestyle changes. I was reading, watching YouTube, and listening to interviews, documentaries, and podcasts for 8 hours a day, for 7 years straight! Pretty soon I had not only healed my autoimmune disease but knew more than the average doctor in the United States about nutrition. Only 25% of US medical schools teach nutrition and it's only one class, so as you can imagine, even doctors were impressed with the information I now had.

In the beginning of my journey, especially as I started seeing fast results, I started warning everyone about the dangers of their dietary choices and lifestyle habits. As you can imagine, no one wanted to hear it! I was still dealing with joint pain, hair loss, skin rashes, and fatigue, why would anyone listen to me! The changes that had started were only on the inside. No one could see the results yet. Keep in mind that not everyone wants a solution.

Years later when my disease was healed and long forgotten from my mind, I had a full head of hair, glowing skin, and had lost a ton of weight, everyone wanted to find out my secrets! In fact, people were willing to pay me money for it. Same information, different levels of embodiment. Lesson learned! Now I embody first and let them pay me for the information if they want it. No spitting out of information or unsolicited coaching!

Another issue with this stage is the inability to surrender and let go of control. This can make relationships really difficult. Even as a coach working with SAB phase two can present some challenges. They come in as a client and often want to rearrange my business or coach me, LOL. At my in-person events, stage two SAB often keeps running out of the room asking hotel staff for this or that. No one asked them to be the help, but they struggle being a guest! Having strong boundaries really helps when dealing with SABs in phase two.

Phase three SAB: This stage is my absolute favorite level to work with! In this stage, our SAB has had some encounters of flow and surrender. She has not quite mastered full energy fluidity like the Million Dollar Babe but the desire has been awakened for more! In this stage, the SAB doesn't need more information, she needs activations and transmissions from an embodied mentor. She needs examples and inspirations. Sort of like a four-minute mile to fully break through her limiting beliefs around femininity, ease, and flow. In fact, in this stage, giving them too much information may trigger them back to stage two.

Our SAB is finally starting to activate her feminine energy in addition to her already cultivated masculine side. She isn't intentional or fully conscious of this yet, but it's definitely a step in the right direction! This stage overlaps with the Million Dollar Babe stage one. If you spend more time in your SAB than your MDB then you are phase three SAB. If you spent more time in your MDB, than your SAB, then you are stage one MDB.

This is the stage I spent my life in from ages 16-33 and the reason I manifested my autoimmune disease. It's like an eternal fight or flight switch turns on and you realize you can't really depend on others around you. Despite massive trauma in my childhood, I didn't have the luxury of becoming a Basic Babe. I didn't trust others to support me in any way. The only option then was to do it all yourself and trust no one. As a feminine essence woman, this became a direct conflict to how I wanted to live and be treated in relationships.

Of course, there is nothing wrong with being resourceful and independent. I still value these traits in myself and others. The issue is that this "I gotta do it all myself and can't trust anyone" attitude is coming from a fight or flight place. About 80% of the women who find my work online are in the Self-Aware Barbie phase three. After serving tens of thousands of women in this stage through my courses and group coaching programs, I have a deep seated knowledge and understanding of the mindsets and behaviors stemming from this consciousness.

Self-Aware Barbies are highly self motivated and high achieving women. I absolutely adore their strong work ethics and success drive. They cross their Ts and dot their Is. They are highly educated and strive to become as humanly successful as they can. All of these are amazing things that I also did. The issue is that since they are doing this from an injured intuition and survival place, they lean on their masculine side at the expense of their feminine side, often burning out and making things way more complicated than needed.

As women when we are in fight or flight, we immediately go into our masculine energy. To make matters more complicated, western society in recent decades has disproportionately started favoring masculine energy traits over feminine energy. In order to create anything beautiful and pleasurable, we need both the masculine and feminine polarities. Not just one.

A baby requires both the egg and the sperm. Money requires both energies, attracting it and keeping it. Business requires both as well, the art form and the structure holding and selling the art form. Life gave us both energies for a reason. Attraction definitely requires polarity. This is true in every romantic relationship, not only heterosexual relationships. All relationships will have one person primarily holding the masculine energy and the other holding the feminine.

Unfortunately, our schools and corporations reward mostly masculine traits such as setting goals, keeping time/space, thinking logically/rationally, creating structures, competing, being accountable, and keeping score. This makes it even easier for Self-Aware Barbies to get stuck in this stage on masculine auto-pilot. Feminine traits such as timelessness, intuition, play, rest, feelings, flow, collaboration, creativity, and enjoying the journey are often seen as lazy or weak. These are the very qualities that add magic to our lives. Feminine traits make life worth experiencing for both men and women.

Masculine energy was a fail safe mechanism in women. We were never designed to be stuck in this mode for long periods of time. We simply don't have the same testosterone as men to be able to run masculine energy in the ways currently expected of us in society. Women who are living mostly in their masculine energy and never have a break to recharge and rest through the feminine end up with all kinds of relationship and health issues. Their general satisfaction and happiness in life also suffers. Which in turn affects their families' well-being.

Lack of romance in relationships, loss of libido, burnout, adrenal fatigue, autoimmune issues, and other deadly diseases are just some of the side-effects of women overusing their masculine energy. I absolutely adore nature for giving us the Self-Aware Barbie stage as an option and beautiful range. When used correctly, this stage is what gives us our resourcefulness, ability to set goals, and see them through. This stage saved my life at a time when I needed it most in my teens and all of my 20s but it also burned me out and caused numerous health and relationship issues.

When I married my husband in 2008, he retired me from my business. I had the perfect chance to rest, rejuvenate, and truly feel safe for the first time in my life. However, because I only knew how to be a Self-Aware Barbie, my nervous system was very restless and unable to adapt to my new pace of life for a long while. I only knew how to be in my masculine energy most of the time. I didn't really know how to enjoy my femininity. Without my business to keep my masculine energy occupied, I started showing up in masculine ways in my marriage. And the romance went out the door pretty quickly at that point because two alphas can't create polarity!

Being in my masculine most of the time also caused a lot of health and other issues. Integrating and evolving out of the SAB stage was honestly the best thing that happened to me! Living primarily in your feminine energy and using your masculine energy in conscious, intentional ways instead of fight or flight is so nourishing!! It makes life seem magical and orgasmic!

Integrating my femininity back into my life made me so much more powerful as a woman. I got healthier, my fibroids, adrenal fatigue, hair loss, skin rashes, and not to mention rheumatoid arthritis, all went away. I honestly credit the Million Dollar Babe stage for my romantic, healthy marriage, great health and energy, happy home, spirituality and all my financial and life success! This is what I help my clients and students do. Integrate the SAB from a healthy place and then move on to the Million Dollar Babe stage.

You are a Self-Aware Barbie, if you...

- Are highly self-motivated and high achieving in your studies and career.
- Need to control everything and need things to be perfect to feel good.
- Feel like no one else can do it like you and therefore often refuse support.
- Can juggle many tasks and to do lists and are always looking to add more things to your plate.
- Have trouble relaxing and resting, there is always so much more to do.
- Often get taken advantage of in relationships because of your over giving and people-pleasing nature.
- Typically outperform the men in your life in basically every area of life.
- Have trouble in romantic relationships because men are intimidated by you.

- Consider yourself and/or are considered by others an Alpha female.
- Look powerful on the outside but often feel weak and scared on the inside.
- Have trouble accessing your emotions and often feel numb to pleasure.

If this is you, you need feminine energy inner work yesterday!! Self-Aware Barbies make the ideal clients and students for my body of work. Through reclaiming your feminine power, nervous system reprogramming, and activating flow states, you become a healed whole being and start to function at full capacity. Imagine learning that one of your hands was tied behind your back all along. You accomplished all that you did with just one arm!! As amazing and admirable as that is, it's also exhausting. I have been there and I know what that burn out feels like. Imagine what you could do and be if all of you were in sync and harmonious. This is what living in alignment truly means.

The reason these two lower stages are becoming more and more common in society right now is because of the absence of maternal presence in the first three years of life. According to Psychoanalyst, Author, and Parent Coach Erica Komisar, there should be as little as possible separation between the mother and baby in the first three years. Babies learn to manage their emotions and place in the world through attunement with their mother in these formative years. The mom not only needs to be physically but also emotionally present for the child to develop in a healthy way mentally and physically. Licensed professional counselor, Kelly McDaniel refers to the absence of loving, safe, maternal presence in these early years as mother hunger, in her book, Mother Hunger.

Modern day parents have been sold the lie of babies needing socialization in daycares and many who are able to stay home decide not to. The child, having been robbed of the attunement with the mother, develops coping mechanisms to deal with life. The Basic Babe becomes hungry for attention and affection, which will resort to creating drama or problems to get attention from anyone, not realizing she internally deeply craves mother 's presence. This may start early on as a toddler throwing tantrums and a child in school unable to focus and learn. The Self-Aware Barbie chooses her achievements, over-giving, over-doing, people-pleasing as her coping mechanism hoping to win the love that was her God-given birthright all along.

This is not to blame mothers but allows parents to make the first three years the most important time for their children's entire life. Finding this research led to a double grieving process in my life. I first had to grieve the loss of not having my mother present and available when I was born, resulting in over 40 years of inner work. I know my mother wanted to be there but my parents needed both incomes and life was stressful for them as immigrants. Secondly, I had to grieve my first son's lack of maternal presence. When Armaan was born, I was in the middle of a very stressful divorce, a student at Northwestern University, and running a real estate business. He rarely had time with me. Contrary to popular belief, quality time is not the same as quantity of time. He needed me there all the time.

Luckily, both my son and I had the luxury of doing inner work because we knew this as an option and solution to not having the essential pair bonding time in the first three years of his life. It makes me sad to think that most people spend their entire life suffering and have no idea inner work was even an option.

I will now share with you the two healed stages of consciousness from my work. Remembering that healed doesn't mean your inner work has ended, inner work happens in layers and there is always room for improvement.

Million Dollar Babe

The Million Dollar Babe is the stage of Feminine/Masculine healing and integration. In this stage, surrender is a natural way of being because we trust in love and feel safe in our body and in the world. The Million Dollar Babe lives in divine flow, utilizing the beautiful structures she has created in her life. Because she is intuitive and fully receptive to her spirit and angel guides, this manifesting babe never feels or works alone. She is fully balanced and fluid in her masculine/feminine energies. This manifesting queen is vulnerable, sensual, and fully embodied in her delicious worthiness. Her heart is fully open and rests in warmth, faith, and love. This is the "lucky bitch" stage where everyone assumes our MDB is just born lucky, not realizing this is a learned and embodied stage and they too can activate it.

In this fully integrated frequency, the left and right sides of the brain are perfectly in sync and working together, giving you what may seem like superhuman abilities. This means you are experiencing moments of what is known as the zone or flow. Since you are perfectly balanced in your feminine and masculine energies, you can switch and sway between the two very easily. This is how we would naturally be if the mother wound hadn't occurred in our early formative years. However, me and my clients and students have had to reparent ourselves to learn this essential way of living and being.

You are a Million Dollar Babe, if you…

- Are able to flow fluidly between your masculine and feminine energies.
- Know how and when to create polarity with your romantic partner.
- Trust that the world is good and the Universe is always working in your favor.
- Have no trouble manifesting your desires and normalizing them once they arrive.
- You are able to create money with ease and flow and exponentially grow your wealth through investing.
- Have a great relationship with your intuition and can make decisions easily.
- Live in your overflow and are able to feel and amplify pleasure in every area of your life.
- Are able to stay in your zone of genius and access flow states, making everything you touch turn to gold.
- Everyone around you thinks you were born lucky because you make everything look effortless and easy.

- Win in relationships because of your strong sense of self and energetic boundaries.
- Don't get triggered very often and know exactly how to process your emotions if you do without having to throw them out on anyone else.

If you identify with this stage, appreciate and enjoy everything you have created while still learning and expanding into more. Healed and whole people like you are essential role models for society. You are contributing to the morphogenetic field for all others around you. You may have your moments of doubt when you surround yourself with people who are suffering, but never feel guilty for what you have and who you are. Your unapologetic light and radiance are necessary ingredients for the healing of all women on this planet, especially at this time. You are the four-minute mile society needs right now, always remember that.

High End Divinity

This is the stage of oneness in all things. In this stage, we move from manifesting it to becoming it. High End Divinity is my word for high priestess. In this stage you are more activated in your consciousness and metaphysical self than in your human animal self. In simple terms, you're able to turn off the amygdala and keep that fight or flight response almost always turned off, increasing your presence in the now. This doesn't mean you spiritually bypass your human experience, but it does mean you are more aware of and connected with the spiritual aspects of your being. You are the observer versus the reactor to most things in life. Which eliminates very high or low emotional waves.

You are a High-End Divinity, if you...

- Have manifested everything you have desired and more for yourself and now want to help others through your overflow.
- Rarely ever get triggered and actually end up helping the people triggering you.
- Give more than you take from the world and the quantum field.

- Are aware of other timelines and lifetimes beyond just this one.
- Are able to jump and collapse timelines at the speed of light.

If you identify with this stage, you have the ability to self-regulate and coach yourself back into alignment and are probably only using me as a peer group grid to collaborate and create with.

Journal Prompts:

Which of the four stages is my dominant stage at this point in my journey?

When you're at your best, are you at the next stage?

What steps will you implement to be more grounded in your current stage or get to the next one?

Additional notes:

PART 2:

KEY LESSONS AND JOURNAL PROMPTS FROM LADY BALLS BOOK

Chapter One:

YOUR DESIRES ARE NOT PROBLEMS

"God has already decided and is showing you a glimpse of a different location in time/space. You are summoned to something bigger and greater, a new possibility awaits. The Universe is not a peasant, and therefore we shouldn't be either!" - Mina Irfan

Lesson: Your Desires are Divine Directions to a different location in time/space where something new and different is available for you. They do not need to be problem solved. Use your desires as previews of what's to come.

Affirmation: *"My desires and pleasures are my gift to humanity."*

Journal Prompts:

What is the deepest desire of my heart right now?

_____

_____

_____

_____

What is the desire I'm not willing to own?

What is the desire I am making wrong in some way?

_____

_____

_____

_____

_____

_____

_____

_____

_____

_____

_____

_____

_____

What desire am I currently treating like a problem to be solved?

What do I truly desire?

Where in my life am I manifesting out and down?

How can I change it to manifesting in and up?

Where in my life am I still manifesting from needs versus desires?

Additional notes:

Chapter Two:

WOMB WOUNDS

> *"I am that powerful single point in the blood line that breaks out of suffering and scarcity, changing my family's morphogenetic field. I am the legacy line breaker. I am the Golden Sheep. I owe it to my ancestors and descendants to live my best life, and so do you!"* - Mina Irfan

Lesson: We now have scientific evidence that proves that trauma is transferred in the womb. Most of our womb wounds come from the mother line. Although we do inherit conditioning from both sides of our lineage. Examine your womb wounds and conditioning unless you are happy to become a replica of your ancestry and closest family and friends.

Affirmation: "It is my God-given right to live life on my own terms."

Journal Prompts:

What are the womb wounds and conditioning I inherited from my mother?

_____

_____

_____

What conditioning did I receive from my father?

What did I learn from other important caregivers or family members?

What did I learn from them about success, money, womanhood?

How are these things still impacting me now in positive or negative ways?

_____

_____

_____

_____

_____

_____

_____

_____

_____

_____

_____

_____

_____

_____

Additional notes:

Chapter Three:

BABES, BARBIES, AND LUCKY BITCHES

"Reading a book doesn't suddenly undo generations of programming trapped in our DNA and cellular memory. We must learn to "overcorrect" by being a savage to land in the happy middle space of healthy relationships with self and others. Being a source of inspiration, power, and abundance on this planet is not only your birthright but also all of ours to witness through your embodiment." - Mina Irfan

Lesson: Some women are born knowing their place in the world, feeling comfortable in their own skin, and confident in navigating the world and setting boundaries. It's hitting the genetic and conditioning lottery jackpot! I was not born that woman and I bet neither were you. However, you can create a new reality by following the savage principles and advice in the Lady Balls book.

Affirmation: *"I'm ready to shed the womb wounds and conditioning to be a successful woman in today's world."*

Journal Prompts:

What wounds and conditioning am I ready to let go of?

What deeply rooted habits do not serve me any more?

What skill sets do I need to obtain to become the special unicorn woman?

In what areas of life am I going to embody more savage power?

Additional notes:

Chapter Four:

EVERYONE IS ADDICTED TO SUFFERING

> *"Evolution takes time. Consciousness does not. So, you can use your conscious awareness to evolve out of our collective pre-programmed addictions to suffering or you can continue being a slave to your brain."* - Mina Irfan

Lesson: Most of your problems are imaginary. Our primitive brain developed in times of extreme hardships. As a result of this programming, we evolved a brain that was massively addicted to suffering. It's not going to suddenly evolve out of millions of years of programming just because we traded jungles for cities. Your brain is still wired to perceive survival threats and worry about them constantly. As modern day homo sapiens, we must use our self-awareness and consciousness to evolve our brain out of this addiction to suffering. This is where inner work comes in.

Affirmation: *"I choose to normalize abundance and prosperity in my life."*

Homework:

Take a sheet of notebook paper and fold it in half vertically.
On one side write down the words: God's job.
On the other side write down: My job.

Now whenever you find yourself swimming in problems, write down what is God's job and what is your job.

Here is an example:

God's Job: *Figure out the solutions and send me signs on which actions to take if any.*	*My Job:* *Keep the faith.*

Take aligned action trusting that God has a plan. Feel good.

Journal Prompts:

Is it hard for me not to jump in and save certain people, or perhaps everyone?

_____

_____

_____

_____

_____

_____

Where does this come from?

What will happen if I don't help? What am I most afraid of? What are the core beliefs underneath this fear?

Are these beliefs serving me?

What new beliefs do I need to embody to get over my overgiving and overdoing tendencies?

What am I currently tempering with that I simply need to "let play out?"

Where was I quick to judge something as a problem because I couldn't see all of its gifts and blessings?

_____

_____

_____

_____

_____

_____

_____

_____

_____

_____

_____

_____

_____

Where in my life am I inviting drama in?

How am I carrying and spreading it around?

Where can I let drama simply starve itself out?

What do I currently worry about that is not my job?

How can I properly outsource those "problems" to others who love solving those exact problems?

What do I consider actual problems in my life?

What am I currently removing emotional energy from?

What are my new, upgraded, elevated "problems" that I enjoy investing time and energy into?

Additional notes:

Chapter Five:

THE HAVING IT ALL BLUEPRINT

> *"Your core beliefs shape your identity and will need to be examined and visited and revisited many times throughout your life. If your identity doesn't match where you are headed, your subconscious won't let you go there. This is why we sabotage our growth."* - *Mina Irfan*

Lesson: Our core beliefs and personal values are automations that help us decide once. Core beliefs are stored in the subconscious and need to be updated as we evolve and grow to match our new identity. Personal values are decisions you make once and then filter all future options through. They make your life streamlined and cohesive and since they are unbendable and the same for all people, it keeps manipulators and users away.

Affirmation: *"Everything is always working out for me. Even if I can't see it at that exact moment."*

Journal Prompts:

What are my current core beliefs? Are they serving me?

_____

_____

Do my current core beliefs need to be updated to match the new identity I am creating for myself?

What are my current personal values? How will these help me decide once and automate?

How will I uphold these decisions for everyone?

In what areas of your life do you need a larger container?

What is the current number from 1 to 10 for this container?

What are the steps you will take to expand your container just a little bit more?

What feminine season of life am I in? What do I need to prioritize in this season?

What needs to be removed from my life currently to truly focus on the most important things?

Do I need to create a customized blueprint for my life? What will that look like?

Additional notes:

Chapter Six:

WOMEN ARE THE GATEKEEPERS OF DNA

"Moms and dads should be dangerous to predators. Let them see us and run in the other direction. Let them cross the street so they don't have to pass by us late at night. Let them shiver and stay up at night worried about what we could do to them if they cross our paths." - Mina Irfan

Lesson: The way things are going in the western dating world, the predators will soon outnumber the providers. And that is not a world I want to leave behind for my children and future descendants. Until very recently, men had to jump through hoops getting an excellent education, making a successful career, impressing a woman's family, and then asking her hand in marriage to be able to have a family. Now a man can pick up a woman at a bar and make a baby with her, over a freaking drink! Savage is not only your birthright but also your service to humanity. People-pleasing, over-giving, and over-doing makes you and your loved ones an open target to manipulators and users. Women must raise their standards by becoming the savage and gatekeeping DNA.

Affirmation: *"I am the most important gate and decision point in the bloodline."*

Journal Prompts:

What feminine lessons did I learn from my earliest caregivers about relationships?

_____

_____

_____

_____

_____

_____

_____

_____

_____

_____

_____

_____

_____

_____

_____

What masculine lessons did I learn from my earliest caregivers about relationships?

What are my new core beliefs around what I get to have in relationships?

What are my new personal values around relationships?

_____

_____

_____

_____

_____

_____

_____

_____

_____

_____

_____

_____

_____

_____

What does a man need to provide to have access to me energetically, emotionally, and sexually?

Additional notes:

Chapter Seven:

BE A BITCH ONCE

"You get to choose how you design your life. Oddly enough, I have preserved way more relationships by Being a Bitch Once than by trying to be nice. Try it, it's a game changer and a savage requirement for the top 1% woman you are destined to become." - Mina Irfan

Lesson: Be a Bitch Once so you don't have to be a bitch many times. Be consistent in your "NOs" and soon enough it will become a part of your identity and you will no longer be seen as a validation seeking junkie and people pleaser! They are not you and you are not them. Give them and their opinions the energetic finger and keep it moving. Decide to actually do something about the negative voices in your head and take action to improve your life.

Affirmation: *"I see everyone as fully capable."*

Homework:

Write out the following statements in your journal and see what comes up. These statements have helped me gain clarity on my new boundaries in life.

"I am no longer available for…"
"I am now open to receive…"

Journal Prompts:

Where in my life did I try playing the nice girl and then end up being a bitch many times?

_____

_____

_____

_____

_____

_____

_____

_____

_____

_____

_____

_____

_____

Where in my life can I Be a Bitch Once so I don't have to be a bitch many times?

_____

_____

_____

_____

_____

_____

_____

_____

_____

_____

_____

_____

How will Being a Bitch Once actually heal and support my relationships?

_____

_____

_____

_____

_____

_____

_____

_____

_____

_____

_____

_____

_____

_____

Who is currently taking up rent free residence in my mind and needs the energetic finger?

What is my internal audience currently saying? How can I listen to it using the self-esteem hack and turn it into my personal cheerleading squad?

What are my current emotional boundaries? Do they serve where I am going or do they need to be updated?

What are my current physical boundaries? Do they serve where I am going
or do they need to be updated?

What are my current energetic boundaries? Do they serve where I am going or do they need to be updated?

Where in my life do I truly need support but am trying to DIY it?

How will having support help me collapse time and quantum leap my progress?

Where in my life am I not allowing or receiving the support I desire?

What would happen if I surrendered to being supported?

Are my current beliefs around support, expanding me or contracting my growth?

Additional notes:

Chapter Eight:

WEALTHY WOMAN ERA BEGINS

"The biggest difference between the Self-Aware Barbie and Million Dollar Babe is embodiment. Embodiment is when the information you have gathered has been memorized by your body. It has become a part of your daily habits, and most importantly, your identity. Instead of knowing the thing, you have become the thing." -
Mina Irfan

Lesson: Between each season of life, there is an intersection of identity. Sometimes women can really struggle at that intersection of identities, for example when they leave the education stage and step into dating for marriage. Each transition brings its own life lessons, challenges, doubts, awakenings, and ascension process. At each phase you may need to revisit your core beliefs and see how they match the new identity you are stepping into. This is the junction at which we tend to self sabotage the most. The muscle memory of the old self often pulls at the consciousness of the self we are becoming. For those of us doing inner work in addition to following our seasons of life, there are additional intersections, the ones between the four stages of consciousness.

Affirmation: *"I'm stepping into my new identity with ease and flow."*

Journal Prompts:

In what ways do I tend to self sabotage my growth? How can I support my nervous system in the transition?

In what ways is my masculine side currently supporting me?

In what ways is my feminine side currently supporting me?

_____

_____

_____

_____

_____

_____

_____

_____

_____

_____

_____

_____

What areas of my life need more feminine energy?

What areas of my life need more masculine energy?

How can these two energies work better together to create a beautiful life experience for me?

_____

_____

_____

_____

_____

_____

_____

_____

_____

_____

_____

_____

_____

Additional notes:

Chapter Nine:

WHEN GOD IS YOUR BUSINESS PARTNER

"A new microphone isn't suddenly going to give you the courage to speak your truth. You have to give yourself permission to be seen and heard first. Work with what you have now, and then improve over time. That is you backing yourself up and truly creating art. Don't let the figuring out stage of something or that new purchase of the right gear stop you from making art with the Divine. I believe true creation is using what we have on hand first and upgrading later as our craft expands.

Qualifying ourselves is about deciding to be enough and the willingness to work with what you currently have. Even if we are still learning, still growing, and may not have all the perfect answers yet. There is someone out there that needs your exact flavor of intelligence delivered in exactly your unique way. Don't make them wait for it." - Mina Irfan

Lesson: Being a heart-centered entrepreneur truly requires you to use both your left brain and right brain and heart and mind in co-creation and divine collaboration. You are going to have to break your addiction to only using the logical side of your brain. The feminine and masculine must work together in divine union in your life and business.

Affirmation: *"God is my algorithm, and Angels do my marketing."*

Homework:

Make a list of all of your current beliefs around money. These are things that you have picked up from parents, siblings, friends, family, teachers, peers, society, and culture. Some are serving you and others not so much.

Now take a moment to look at them. Right there in black and white. Innocently staring back at you. These are your current belief systems. Which of these would you intentionally choose for yourself? Those are the ones you get to keep. For the ones that feel icky - let's work through them. Are they ultimate, absolute truths? Are they true for everyone on the planet? Are they things that the highest most loving cosmic forces would want for you?

Rewrite them into NEW, Upgraded, Core Beliefs. These will be your NEW beliefs that you will affirm thousands of times a day with high emotional states until they become a part of your genetic makeup. Every part of your cell. These beliefs should be oozing out of your pores, as every part of you celebrates and affirms this new way of thinking, feeling, and being!

Journal Prompts:

What was my mother's feminine relationship with money? What was her masculine relationship with money?

What was my father's feminine relationship with money? What was his masculine relationship with money?

What did I learn from both of them? How did this form my own relationship and beliefs around money?

Are my current money struggles more in the feminine manifesting realms or in the masculine keeping and having it realm?

What are my current core beliefs around money? Do these beliefs serve my next level relationship with money?

What new core beliefs do I need to embody to create a new level of money identity?

Additional notes:

Chapter Ten:

LADY BALLS, FEMININE POWER

> *"I have had the pleasure of taking the best from both cultures. From my western culture, I have learned to be independent, set healthy boundaries, and have a strong work ethic. From my eastern side, I have learned to value interdependence, traditions, and relationships. Adding this all up has created a harmonious lifestyle where I truly do get to have it all." - Mina Irfan*

Lesson: Always remember that you are a woman and in a female body. Honor and respect the inner and outer workings of this divine gift you have been given. God had a plan for you when you manifested in exactly this way. Male power comes from their outward strength as a result of 15 folds more testosterone circulating through their systems than women and children. The lifestyle western culture now expects all of us to live is something even men can barely survive. Feminine Power comes from her inner strength, resilience, and range. Feminine Power is solid on the inside and soft on the outside.

Affirmation: *"I am the human manifestation of the Divine Feminine herself and I get to win in every situation."*

Journal Prompts:

What does success mean to me? What are my priorities in life?

In what areas of life am I not willing to settle for less?

What lifestyle would I desire if I turned down the noise of society and its expectations?

How connected am I to my femininity? What can help me reclaim more of that power?

How can I cultivate my feminine part?

How can I cultivate my masculine part?

What skill sets would support me to succeed in relationships?

In what areas of life do I currently need to expand my container?

Additional notes:

PART 3:
EXERCISES AND INVOCATIONS

END THE STRUGGLE INNER WORK
THE 6 STEP PROCESS

1. What is the distortion that my mind is creating? What is the old story? Is this ultimately true?

2. Say the following Surrender Prayer:

"Dear God, please help me release the distortions and lies my mind is creating. I am willing to see things differently. Please help me see and accept new, upgraded, high vibration realities."

3. What is the NEW, Upgraded Truth or Belief system that I am ready to embody? Write out the new story for yourself in your journal.

4. Now close your eyes and spend 2-3 minutes imaging yourself living out the new story. Notice all the details. How are you carrying yourself? How are you speaking? Do you move and/or sound differently? What are you wearing? Is your energy and vibration different? Notice and record this as a movie so you can play it in your mind often.

5. Affirm new beliefs by saying "I Am..." statements with as much feeling as possible. The feeling part is essential! Repetition and High Emotion is what programs the subconscious mind. The higher the emotion, the less repetition is needed. Here are some statements to get you started.

"I Am Worthy."

"I Am Enough."

"I Am Wealthy."

"I Am Healthy."

6. Repeat the new statements with feelings of new core beliefs millions of times until the subconscious memorizes new truths and belief systems. Remember, the higher the emotional state when you feel into your new core beliefs, the less repetition is needed.

RELEASING SHAME AND GUILT EXERCISE

Prayer:

"Dear God, Universe, Angels, I release all guilt and shame. Please transmute all distortions into love and free me from all mental and energetic constraints."

Inner Work Prompt:

Write down *"I feel guilty for..."* and *"I feel shame when..."* Then write down the limiting beliefs that accompany that guilt or shame. Work through those LIES using the six step process given above.

Choose new, more empowering beliefs for yourself!! There are always deeper layers to guilt and shame and once you can work through and reframe them, they no longer mean anything to you.

Affirmations:

"I am now free."

"I am now healed from all shame and guilt."

"I now release all shame and guilt."

This simple process will start to unravel old neural pathways and build new ones matching your new way of being. It also expands your nervous system into holding more higher states of being.

CORE BELIEFS EXERCISE

Set a 10-minute timer on your phone.

Then without lifting your pen off your paper, keep writing the following statement and finishing it with your new empowering core beliefs.

"I choose to know and believe..."

For example:

"I choose to know and believe that everything is always working out for me, even when I can't see it."

"I choose to know and believe that I am healed and whole now."

"I choose to know and believe that my desires are God's plan."

"I choose to know and believe that my existence is a gift to humanity."

"I do these exercises every morning and it has been life changing!"

MINA IRFAN'S EMBODIMENT PROCESS

1. State your desire.

What do I truly desire to embody?

2. Core beliefs.

Does anything need updating for me to be able to embody this?

How does this fit into my personal values?

What parts of my identity need to be updated?

What energy do I need to have for this to be my new reality?

What do I need to get rid of from my life for this to have the space that it needs?

What daily actions do I need to take?

How can I break this down into small, digestible steps that compound over time?

What is the high hanging fruit here that gives me elite level, top 1% advantage?

3. Repeat consistently for long periods of time.

ELEVATOR EMBODIMENT EXERCISE

Close your eyes. Imagine there is an elevator in your head. Notice that it says you are on the 10th floor. Get into the elevator and hit the basement button. Slowly go vertically down your body until the elevator stops and opens in your womb space.

Get out and look around. What do you notice? How do you feel? Are the sensations here different from the 10th floor? Refrain from accessing your brain to answer any of these questions.

You left your brain on the 10th floor. You are now in the basement.

During the day – anytime you find yourself getting too "heady" – take the elevator down and access the womb's wisdom to make your decisions.

Journal on the sensations and inner workings.

SURRENDER PRAYER

Find moments in your day to say the surrender prayer. Say it when you feel overwhelmed, worried, anxious, or just need an extra boost.

"Dear God/Universe/Angels, I surrender to you all my problems, worries, fears, and ask for guidance. Please show me how to release all fears and embody love today. I hand over this problem to you. I am willing to do my part, please show me the way. Thank You."

INTUITION EXERCISE

Take a couple of deep breaths and get into a relaxed state. Ask your intuition a simple question. Nothing too complicated or layered to start with. I started with, "What color should I wear today?" And then drop any expectation of HOW the answer will be delivered to you. Get silent and the answer will come in a split internal knowing through one or the combination of senses.

Don't overthink this process. It's not a mental exercise. If nothing comes through, try again later with a different question. These things often take practice to unlock so never get disheartened if it doesn't work the first time around. You are creating a relationship with your intuition and like any relationship, it can take time to build trust and respect.

CORD CUTTING EXERCISE

TO RESTORE YOUR LIFE FORCE ENERGY LOST THROUGH SEXUAL ENCOUNTERS

This is my cord cutting invocation. Invocations are 21-day rituals that we perform with the aid of our guides, angels, and God. This ritual can help us to restore our energy after encounters with difficult or toxic people. It can also help break generational curses, or sexual entanglements. Please note that this ritual does not replace the therapy most women need after having sexual encounters with men before marriage.

Recite this for 21 days. If you miss a day, start the 21 day count again. I personally love to light a candle and call upon my guides and angels to assist me before I start reciting this. It really helps to recite this daily at about the same time. Within an hour of the same time is okay.

"Dear Divine (God, Universe, Source, Higher Self),

I call upon my loving ancestors, my personal guides, Angels, and God to assist me in this cord cutting ritual.

Dear Divine, I am now released of any ties, cords, entanglements, soul contracts, and vows that no longer serve me.

Dear Divine, I now return back to sender what is not mine.

I now call back all and any missing parts of myself back home.

Please restore my energy to its original soul blueprint as intended at my soul's origination.

Dear Divine, I am now healed and whole in all directions of time and space.

Please cleanse my energy and restore every cell in my body with your golden divine light.

I am now cleansed and renewed with golden divine light.

And so it is!"

21 DAY MONEY CORD CUTTING INVOCATION

Use this Invocation specially for cord cutting around distorted money beliefs.

"Dear Divine/Universe/Creator/God,

Please help me release with grace all cords, vows, contracts, ties, resentments and fears of others from this lifetime and past.

Please clear every cell with LOVE and set me free from all entanglements from the past, present, and future and in all directions of time and space.

I now FORGIVE all, including myself and radiate only LOVE.

I now release what no longer serves me and begin with a clear slate.

I now come home to Divine and Magical Love, Abundance, Radiance, Presence and Faith.

I now remember that I AM an abundant being and always was.

I was born rich and have access to unlimited God Supply for all my desires and more.

I believe with every cell in my body that God will never run out and therefore neither will I!

I am rich. I am abundant. I am wealthy.

Thank you. And so it is!"

ADDITIONAL RESOURCES

Mina Irfan has over 60 digital courses available on her website at www.theuniverseguru.com in topics ranging from inner work, personal power, dating, relationships, parenting, health, and wealth.

She is also the Author of Contained in Love: Reclaiming Your Feminine Power as a Wife and Mother and Lady Balls: How to be Savagely Successful in a World Addicted to Suffering.

To start your inner work, consider the Basic Babe Bundle: https://bit.ly/2HOtbpk

Mina Irfan is the author of best-selling books **Lady Balls** and **Contained in Love**, as well as over 60 digital courses. Her brutal honesty and tough love style is adored by her hundreds of thousands of students globally.

Mina has mentored some of the world's most high performance, high achieving women. Her teachings are a combination of spiritual energy work plus her studies of Communications, Anthropology, and Evolutionary Psychology from Northwestern University.

www.theuniverseguru.com

Made in the USA
Coppell, TX
23 January 2024

28051066R00129